Times of Babylon

The Throne Series

Rabia Farheen

Syed M. Salman Raza Bukhari

About Authors

Rabia Farheen is an Electrical and Electronics Engineer. She was born in Pakistan's Lahore city. She is quite interested in researching the advancement of technology, as well as the cultures and civilizations of many regions. She enjoys exploring new places and was motivated to create wonderful and stunning handmade and digital calligraphy paintings by her interest in calligraphy and painting.

Electrical Engineer **Hafiz Syed M. Salman Raza Bukhar**i is from Pakistan. He studies software and digital design as well. Together with Rabia, he created digital calligraphy and was motivated to work on Digital Calligraphy, the history of many cultures, technological advancements, and people's lives in various areas by his interest in art and culture. He creates wallpaper as well as digital apps and websites..

About Book

Readers can learn about the ancient city of Babylon and the kings' and people's way of life there. People can learn about the cultural situations of Babylon after reading this book. People can learn about a king's stance toward war and policies. People might also learn the fundamental rules of ancient Babylon.

People can comprehend the causes of the Babylonian Empire's rise and demise after reading this book.

Dedication

Thank you Dear God Almighty for giving us the courage and everything in our life.
We want to thank our parents, friends and teachers for being with us and to support us in every situation.
Thank you so much to encourage and guide us in every task of life. You have always stand with us and make us realized that we are not alone and there is something special in us.
Thank you so much Sheikh Muhammad Ibraheem who encouraged us to become authors.

"Dedicated to our beloved ones"

Table of Contents

Chapter 1

Babylon Etymology

The word "Babylon" is a Latinized version of the Greek word "Babylon," which is derived from the native (Babylonian) word "Babilim," which means "gate of the god(s)". It is becoming more common knowledge that the "gate of god" explanation is a Semitic folk etymology (Folk etymology, sometimes referred to as popular etymology, analogical reformation, reanalysis, morphological reanalysis, or etymological reinterpretation, is the process by which an unfamiliar form gets replaced with a more familiar one, changing the meaning of a word or phrase.

Ancient Babylonian Language on Stone

An antique, foreign, or otherwise unknown term is reinterpreted as having similarities to more well-known words or morphemes) used to explain an unknown original non-Semitic place name. As there were other locations in Sumer with names akin to Babilla and there are no other examples of Sumerian (the language of ancient Sumer), Gelb suggested that the original n or Babilla was of unknown origin and meaning in 1955. Place names are being replaced with their Akkadian equivalents. Sumerian is thought to be an isolated language that was spoken in ancient Mesopotamia, commonly known as the Fertile Crescent, in the region that is today Iraq.

That the Sumerian term Kan-digirak was a loan translation of the Semitic folk etymology and not the original name, and that it eventually changed into the Akkadian Bb-ili. The Third Dynasty of Ur's (The Third Dynasty of Ur, sometimes known as the Neo-Sumerian Empire, was a short-lived territorial-political entity that some historians believe to have been a fledgling empire. It was centered in the city of Ur and ruled from the 22nd to the 21st century BC (middle chronology). When discussing the Third Dynasty of Ur, historians frequently refer to it as Ur III. It is numbered in relation to earlier dynasties, such as the First Dynasty of Ur (26–25th century BC), although it appears the Second Dynasty of Ur, which was formerly thought to have existed, was never documented.)"Neo-Sumerian" period would have seen the re-translation of the Semitic name into Sumerian.

The term Babel is found in the Hebrew Bible (Hebrew: Bavel, Tiberian: Bél; Classical Syriac: Bwl, Aramaic: Bél; in Arabic: Bbil), and is translated as "confusion" in the Book of Genesis from the verb bilbél, which means "to confuse." It is a common misconception that this term is the origin of the contemporary English verb to babble, which means "to speak foolish, excited, or confusing talk" although there is no actual relationship. In certain cases, ancient records refer to other towns as "Babylon," including ones like Borsippa (On the east bank of the Euphrates, 17.7 kilometers (11.0 miles) southwest of Babylon, was an important ancient Sumerian city called Borsippa) that were under Babylon's rule and Nineveh (For around fifty years, it held the title of biggest city in the world. However, in 612 BC, during a bloody period of Assyrian civil conflict, a coalition of its former subjects, including the Babylonians, Medes, Persians, Scythians, and Cimmerians, sacked it. Despite never serving as a governmental or administrative hub again, the city was home to a Christian bishop by Late Antiquity. In comparison to Mosul, it suffered during the middle Ages, and by the 13th century AD, it had mostly been abandoned) for a brief time following the Assyrian conquest of Babylon.

Chapter 2

The First Attested

Early records of Babylon date to the late third millennium BC, under the leadership of Shar-Kali-Sharri of the Akkadian Empire, one of whose year names commemorates the construction of two temples there. Ensi (governors) for the empire oversaw Babylon. Governors like Abba, Ari-a, Itr-ilum, Murteli, Unabatal, and Puzur-Tutu were some of the well-known ones. Nothing further is said about the city after then until Sumu-la-El. Amorite kingdoms start to emerge in southern Uruk and Larsa after around 1950 BC.

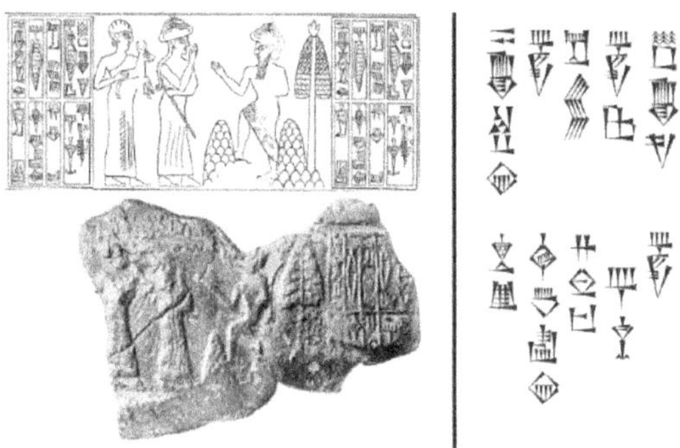

Ancient Carving of stone showing Lugal-ushumgal as servant of Shar-Kali-Sharri

King Shar-Kali-Sharri of the Akkadian Empire ruled from 2217 to 2193 BC (middle chronology) and 215 to 2129 BC (short chronology). In 2217 BC, he succeeded his father Naram-Sin and ascended to the throne at a period of escalating difficulties. He had to deal with a series of vassal king rebellions against the heavy taxes they were made to pay to support the defence against the Gutian menace as the Gutian, who had established a capital at Adab, were conducting increasingly regular attacks. According to modern year-names for Shar-kali-sharri of Akkad, during one of his unnamed years of rule, he defeated the Guterian king Sharlag and "the yoke was put on Gutium" in another year.

Although the governor of Lagash, Lugal-Ushumgal (was a Lagash ("Shirpula") Sumerian ensi (formerly spelled "Patesi") ruler who lived between 2230 and 2210 BCE. Many of Lugal-inscriptions, ushumgal's notably seal impressions, have been discovered. They describe him as the governor of Lagash and, concurrently, as a vassal (arad, "servant" or "slave") of the kings of the Akkadian Empire, Naram-Sin and his successor Shar-Kali-Sharri. Both Meskigal, the king of Adab, and Lugalushumgal might be seen as as collaborators of the Akkadian Empire. Puzer-Mama, who gained independence from Shar-Kali-Sharri and ascended to the throne as "King of Lagash," succeeded him, ushering in the glorious Second Dynasty of Lagash.), declared himself to be a subordinate of Shar-Kali-Sharri, Puzer-Mama (Around 2200 BCE, Puzer-Mama ruled Lagash before Gudea. Puzer-Mama exhibits affinity with later Lagashite rulers in his inscritions while adopting the title of King (lugal). When problems with the Guti left the Sargonic monarch in charge of "a small rump kingdom whose centre was at the junction of the Diyala and Tigris River," this happened during Shar-kali-rule. Share's Puzer-royal Mama's inscription calls on the gods to punish anybody who changes his inscriptions, in particular to "tear out his foundations and annihilate his descendants." He is granted many gifts from the gods suited to his position of authority by Ningirsu. One of the protective curses mentioned in royal inscriptions dating back to Sargon's rule) eventually took over Lagash after the Sargonic monarch was reduced to ruling "a tiny residual kingdom whose centre was at the confluence of the Diyala and Tigris River." The second Lagash dynasty was established by Puzer-Mama.

About 18 of his 24 years of rule are represented by names, which show that he waged victorious wars against the Gutians, Amorites, and Elamites and built temples in Nippur and Babylon. At Akshak, the Elamites were defeated, according to Shar-Kali-Sharri.

During Shar-Kali-rule Sharri's in Sumer, about 2200 BC, the region also experienced a devastating drought that forced the total evacuation of several cities. This is in addition to

Egyptian sources, which indicate that a drought may have occurred around the same period during King Pepi II's reign. After the passing of Shar-Kali-Sharri in around 2193 BC, Sumer descended into disorder, with no ruler able to maintain power for very long.

Dudu, whose reign is estimated to have lasted 21 years according to the king list, was the second documented king of Akkad to hold power for a substantial period of time. Shar-Kali-Sharri was the last Akkadian monarch to truly rule over an empire because at this point the Akkadian kingdom had vanished and Dudu probably just governed Akkad city. Assyriologists mistakenly believed Shar-Kali-Sharri and the Sargon of Agade from Assyrian mythology in the 1870s, but this assumption was disproved in the 1910s.

Chapter 3
Early Age of Babylon

A Babylonian date list states that Sumu-abum, a chieftain who declared his country's independence from the nearby city-state of Kazallu, signalled the beginning of Amorite dominance in Babylon (about the 19th or 18th century BC). Typically, Sumu-la-El is cited as the founder of the First Babylonian dynasty despite the possibility that his dates overlap with those of Sumu-abum. Both are credited for constructing Babylon's walls. Throughout any event, the records speak of Sumu-la-military El's triumphs creating a zone of influence for Babylon in the region.

Amorite Ancient writings on stones

Sumu-Abum (sometimes spelled Su-abu) was an Amorite and the first monarch of Babylon's First Dynasty (the Amorite Dynasty). The official language used at that time was, Akkadian Sumerian and Amorite were local languages. According to a condensed chronology, he ruled from 1830 to 1817 BC, or 1897 to 1883 BC (middle chronology). He liberated a tiny region of territory that had been governed by the neighbouring Amorite city-state of Kazallu, which at the time comprised Babylon, a minor administrative hub in southern Mesopotamia. Sumu-Abum (and the three Amorite kings who followed him) do not identify themselves as the rulers of Babylon, indicating that the city was still of minor significance at the period. It is known that he rose to power and ruled Kisurra.

From the early 21st century BC to the end of the 17th century BC, the Amorites, a prehistoric Northwest Semitic-speaking people from the Levant, also controlled a sizable portion of southern Mesopotamia. During this time, they founded several important city-states in already-existing locations, including Isin, Larsa, and most notably Babylon, which was transformed from a small town into an independent state and a major city. The Amorites, their chief god, and a kingdom are all referred to as Amurru in Akkadian and Sumerian writings. Both before and after Joshua's conquest of the area, the Amorites are referenced in the Bible as residents of Canaan. Beginning around 2400 BC, the oldest Sumerian records on the Amorites refer to their homeland as "the Mar.tu country," which is connected with the regions west of the Euphrates, encompassing Canaan and what would later become Syria, then known as The land of the Amurru and subsequently as Aram and Eber-Nari.

In early Mesopotamian texts from Sumer, Akkad, and Assyria, to the west of the Euphrates, they are described as an uncultured and nomadic people. In Sumerian, Akkadian, and Ancient Egyptian, they were referred to as Mar.tu ("Westerners"), Amurru (said to be descended from aburru, "pasture"), and Amor, respectively. A large-scale migration of Amorite tribes invaded southern Mesopotamia commencing in the 21st century BC, presumably brought on by a protracted significant drought that began around 2200 BC. The Amorite dynasties not only usurped the long-existing local city-states like Isin, Larsa, Eshnunna, and Kish, but they were also one of the factors in the collapse of the Third Dynasty of Ur. Although it was first a little unimportant state, but also founded new ones, the most renowned of which was to become Babylon.

A dialect of Akkadian used by the known Amorites was discovered on tablets from Mari that date from 1800–1750 BC. The Amorite language is a Northwest Semitic language and may even be a Canaanite language because it exhibits northwest Semitic forms, vocabulary, and constructions. The proper names that are retained in such texts—which are not written in the Akkadian phonology—are the primary resource for the extremely scant existing knowledge of the Amorite language. As with the Eblaite of the northern Levant, the Akkadian language of Mesopotamia's native Semitic states, towns, and polities (Akkad, Assyria, Babylonia, Isin, Kish, Larsa, Ur, Nippur, Uruk, Eridu, Adab, Akshak, Eshnunna, Nuzi, etc.) was an east Semitic language.

The First Babylonian Empire, also known as the Old Babylonian Empire, lasted from around 1894 BC to 1595 BC. It occurred following the end of Sumerian dominance with the axing of the Third Dynasty of Ur and the ensuing Isin-Larsa era. Since there is a Babylonian King List A and a Babylonian King List B, the chronology of the first dynasty of Babylonia is up for question. The regnal years of List A are utilised in this chronology owing of their widespread use. In general, the reign durations shown in List B are longer.

Since Babylon itself produces relatively few complete archaeological artefacts due to a high water table, it is difficult to establish the First Babylonian dynasty's exact origins. Thus, written records like as royal and votive inscriptions, literary writings, and lists of year names are among the kind of evidence that have endured over time. It is challenging to depict the First Babylonian Dynasty's economic and social history due to the scant evidence in economic and legal documents, but a chronology may be established thanks to literary depictions of historical events and the availability of year-name lists. Sumuabum, the first monarch of the Dynasty who is known to exist, is credited for expanding Babylonian territory by capturing Dilbat and Kish. Sumualailum, his successor, was able to finish building the wall surrounding Babylon that Sumuabum had started. Additionally, Sumualailum was effective in destroying Kazallu and quelling uprisings in Kish. He even briefly had control of Nippur (though it did not last). Few details are known about the reigns of Sabium, Apil-Sin, and Sin-muballit, other than the fact that they continued to rule the captured land, consolidated the walls, and started constructing canals. Sin-muballit is renowned for his victories over Rim-Sin I. From future assault, Babylon was shielded by Sin-muballit. The kingship would thereafter be transferred from Sin-muballit to his son Hammurabi.

Chapter 4

Era of King Hammurabi

From from 1792 BC until approximately 1750 BC, Hammurabi, the sixth monarch of the Amorite tribe's First Babylonian dynasty, ruled (according to the Middle Chronology). His father, Sin-Muballit, who stepped down due to declining health, came before him. He overthrew Elam as well as the city-states of

Hammurabi King of Babylon

Larsa, Eshnunna, and Mari during his rule. He deposed Assyrian king Ishme-Dagan I and had his son Mut-Ashkur pay tribute, thereby putting all of Mesopotamia under Babylonian power.

The Code of Hammurabi, which Hammurabi claimed to have received from Shamash, the

Babylonian deity of justice, is his most famous work. The Law of Hammurabi was one of the earliest legal codes to lay more emphasis on the physical punishment of the offender, in contrast to earlier Sumerian legal codes like the Code of Ur-Nammu, which had placed more emphasis on compensating the victim of the crime. It was one of the earliest regulations to establish the presumption of innocence and defined particular punishments for each offence. Although its punishments are severe by today's standards, they were created to restrict what a wronged person may do in retaliation. There are several parallels between the Torah's Law of Moses and the Hammurabi Code.

Within his own lifetime, Hammurabi was revered by many as a deity. Hammurabi was regarded as a great conqueror who spread civilization and made all peoples worship Marduk, the deity of the Babylonians, after his death. Later, his military successes lost importance, and his reputation as the perfect lawmaker took over as the main part of his legacy. Later Mesopotamians used Hammurabi's rule as the standard for all things that happened in the distant past. Many rulers throughout the Near East claimed him as an ancestor, even after the kingdom he founded fell to ruin. He was still regarded as a perfect leader.

Around 1792 BC, Hammurabi, an Amorite First Dynasty monarch of the city-state of Babylon, succeeded his father Sin-Muballit. One of the many city-states that dot the central and southern Mesopotamian plains and are predominately dominated by Amorites, Babylon was one of these cities that fought each other for control of rich agricultural territory. Although many other civilizations coexisted in Mesopotamia, it was under Hammurabi that Babylonian culture rose to prominence among the Middle Eastern literary classes. In 1894 BC, the monarchs who came before Hammurabi established the little City State, which had limited power outside of the city. For around a century after its creation, Babylon was overshadowed by older, bigger, and more powerful kingdoms like Elam, Assyria, Isin, Eshnunna, and Larsa. However, under the reign of his father Sin-Muballit, the petty city-states of Borsippa, Kish, and Sippar had already been subjugated by Babylonian hegemony in a limited region of south central Mesopotamia. So, amid a complicated geopolitical setting, Hammurabi came to rule as the ruler of a small state. Eshnunna, a strong monarchy, ruled over the upper Tigris River, and Larsa ruled over the river delta. The strong kingdom of Elam, which was east of Mesopotamia, frequently attacked the lesser nations of southern Mesopotamia and exacted tribute from them. The Assyrian monarch Shamshi-Adad I of northern Mesopotamia had expanded his realm into the Levant and central Mesopotamia after inheriting centuries-old Assyrian colonies in Asia Minor, yet his unexpected death would slightly destabilise his kingdom.

The early years of Hammurabi's rule were rather quiet. Hammurabi exercised his authority to carry out a number of public projects, such as raising the city walls for defence and enlarging the temples. Approximately 1701 BC saw the invasion of the Mesopotamian plain by the strong kingdom of Elam, which straddled significant trade routes through the Zagros Mountains. Elam attacked and subdued the kingdom of Eshnunna with the aid of the states of the plain, obliterating a number of cities and for the first time establishing its dominance over parts of the plain. Elam attempted to incite conflict between the kingdom of Larsa and the kingdom of Hammurabi in order to strengthen its position. Although Larsa did not significantly assist to the military effort, Hammurabi and the king of Larsa formed an alliance after learning of this deceit and were able to defeat the Elamites. By around 1763 BC, Hammurabi had taken control of the whole lower Mesopotamian plain after turning against Larsa, who had failed to help him out of anger.

The lack of soldiers in the north caused dissatisfaction since Yamhad and Mari, two of Hammurabi's supporters from the north, supported him throughout the battle in the south. Hammurabi switched his focus northward as he expanded, putting an end to the disturbance and swiftly destroying Eshnunna. The remaining northern nations were afterwards subdued by the Babylonian troops, including Mari, which was once an ally of Babylon. However, it's likely that Mari's conquest was only a submission without any actual combat.

For control of Mesopotamia, Hammurabi and Ishme-Dagan I of Assyria engaged in a lengthy battle in which both monarchs formed alliances with lesser powers to obtain the upper hand. Ishme-Dagan I was eventually overthrown by Hammurabi, who did so soon before his own demise. The new king of Assyria, Mut-Ashkur, was compelled to give Hammurabi tribute.

Hammurabi was able to unify Mesopotamia under his reign in a few of years. Only Aleppo and Qatna to the west in the Levant preserved their independence out of the major city-states in the area, while the Assyrian monarchy endured but was compelled to pay tribute during his rule. Hammurabi does, however, claim to be "King of the Amorites" on one of his steles, which has been discovered as far north as Diyarbekir.

Numerous contract tablets from Hammurabi's and his successors' eras, as well as 55 of his own letters, have been uncovered. These letters offer a peek into the struggles of governing an empire on a daily basis, including managing floods, ordering corrections to an inaccurate calendar, and tending to Babylon's enormous herds of cattle. Around 1750 BC saw the death of Hammurabi and the transfer of the throne to his son Samsu-iluna, whose tenure saw the rapid disintegration of the Babylonian empire.

Chapter 5

The Codes of Hammurabi

The System of Ur-Nammu, which is the oldest known legal code still in existence today, predates the Code of Hammurabi as the oldest surviving legal code. The Laws of Eshnunna (found engraved on two cuneiform tablets at Tell Ab Harmal, Baghdad, Iraq), the Code of Lipit-Ishtar, and it is from Mesopotamia and is

Codes of hammurabi

written on tablets in the Sumerian language between 2100 and 2050 BCE. However, the Code of Hammurabi differs substantially from these earlier legal systems and eventually turned out to be more significant.

Despite the fact that it is believed that few people were literate, the Code of Hammurabi was engraved on a Stele and set up in a public area where everyone could read it. After being looted by the Elamites and transported to their capital city of Susa, the stele was subsequently found in Iran and is currently on display at the Louvre Museum in Paris. The 282 regulations included in Hammurabi's code were inscribed by scribes on 12 tablets. It was written in Akkadian, the daily language of Babylon, unlike prior rules, and anybody with literacy in the city could read it.

The Code of Hammurabi, in contrast to earlier Sumerian legal systems, placed more emphasis on the corporal punishment of the criminal. One of the earliest legal texts to limit what a mistreated person may do in retaliation was the Code of Hammurabi.

Each transgression carries a corresponding punishment according to the code's highly detailed structure. By contemporary standards, the penalties were often exceedingly severe, with many transgressions leading to death, physical harm, or the application of the "Eye for eye, tooth for tooth" (Lex Talionis "Law of Retaliation") principle.

The rule also says that both the accuser and the accused have the chance to present evidence, making it one of the first examples of the presumption of innocence. Extenuating factors are not allowed to change the mandatory sentence, nevertheless.

The preamble indicates that Shamash chose Hammurabi to convey the rules to the people, and a sculpture at the top of the stele shows Hammurabi receiving the laws from Shamash, the Babylonian deity of justice. Similarities between the two legal codes and parallels between this story and the biblical Book of Exodus' account of Yahweh handing Moses the Covenant Code on Mount Sinai imply that the two legal systems have a Semitic ancestor.

Even Nevertheless, pieces of earlier legal systems have been discovered, making it doubtful that the Mosaic rules were influenced directly by the Code of Hammurabi. David P. Wright asserts that the Jewish Covenant Code is "directly, principally, and entirely" based on the Laws of Hammurabi, in contrast to those academics who contest this. A group of archaeologists from Hebrew University found a cuneiform tablet in Hazor in Israel in 2010 that was written in the eighth or seventh century BC and contained regulations that were unmistakably taken from the Code of Hammurabi.

During the rule of Hammurabi, Babylon usurped Nippur's title as the "most sacred city" in southern Mesopotamia. The short-lived Babylonian Empire started to disintegrate under the leadership of Hammurabi's successor Samsu-iluna. Around 1740 BC, the native

Akkadian-speaking monarch Puzur-Sin expelled the Amorites and Babylonians from Assyria in northern Mesopotamia. The Sealand Dynasty was established in roughly the same area as ancient Sumeria at the same time local Akkadian speakers overthrew Amorite Babylonian authority in the extreme south of Mesopotamia.

Assyrian rulers like Adasi and Bel-ibni, as well as the Sealand Dynasty to the south, Elam to the east, and the Kassites from the northeast, dealt more defeats and territorial losses to Hammurabi's ineffective successors. As a result, Babylon was swiftly reduced to the little, insignificant state it had been before its creation.

The mighty Hittite Empire stormed and destroyed Babylon in 1595 BC, terminating the Amorite political presence in Mesopotamia and delivering the death blow to the Amorite Dynasty of Hammurabi. But the Indo-European-speaking Hittites abandoned Babylon and handed it over to their Kassite allies from the Zagros Mountains, who spoke an isolated language. For more than 400 years, the Kassite Dynasty governed Babylon and incorporated many parts of Babylonian civilization, notably Hammurabi's code of laws.

But even after the Amorite Dynasty was overthrown, Hammurabi was still regarded with awe. Shutruk-Nahhunte I of Elam conquered Babylon in 1158 BC and took several stone monuments with him. He had the majority of the inscriptions on these monuments removed and new ones inscribed into them. However, just four or five columns on the stele carrying Hammurabi's rules were removed, and no new writing was ever inserted. The rulers of Suhu, a region on the Euphrates River northwest of Babylon, claimed Hammurabi as their ancestor more than a thousand years after his passing. The intense Babel und Bibel ("Babylon and Bible") debate in Germany over the connection between the Bible and ancient Babylonian texts made the Code of Hammurabi a significant topic of discussion in the late nineteenth century. The German Assyriologist Friedrich Delitzsch asserted in a speech delivered in front of the Kaiser and his wife in January 1902 at the Sing-Akademie zu Berlin that the Mosaic Laws of the Old Testament were directly derived from the Code of Hammurabi.

In response to this lecture and the one before it about the Flood tale in the Epic of Gilgamesh, Delitzsch was able to gather 1,350 short pieces from newspapers and magazines, over 300 lengthier ones, and twenty-eight booklets by the end of September 1903. Although a handful of these pieces were sympathetic, the most of them were negative of Delitzsch. Delitzsch was compelled to deliver his third lecture in Cologne and Frankfurt am Main rather than Berlin in the fall of 1904 as a result of the Kaiser's distancing himself from him and his radical viewpoints. The alleged connection between the Mosaic Law and the Code of Hammurabi later became a key component of Delitzsch's argument in his 1920–1921 book Die grobe Täuschung (The Great Deception) that the Hebrew Bible was inherently tainted by Babylonian influence and that Christians could only finally accept the true, Aryan message of the New Testament by completely eradicating the human Old Testament.

Many academics thought that Hammurabi was Amraphel, the King of Shinar described in Genesis 14:1, during the beginning of the twentieth century. Since Amraphael's presence is not mentioned in any non-Biblical texts, this theory has been substantially disproved.Given Hammurabi's status as a legislator, there are several American political structures that feature his likeness. One of the 23 legislators shown in marble bas-reliefs in the U.S. House of Representatives chamber in the United States Capitol is Hammurabi. On the south wall of the U.S. Supreme Court building is a frieze by Adolph Weinman that features Hammurabi and other "great lawgivers of history." The 1st Hammurabi Armoured Division of the Iraqi Army was given the name of the ancient king during the reign of Saddam Hussein in an effort to highlight the similarities between contemporary Iraq and the pre-Arab Mesopotamian cultures.

Chapter 6
King Samsu-iluna

Samsu-iluna, also known as Shamshu and reigning from around 1750 to 1712 BC (according to the middle chronology), or from 1686 to 1648 BC, was the seventh king of the founding Amorite dynasty of Babylon (short chronology). He was the heir of Hammurabi and the son of an unidentified woman. His rule was characterized by the bloody uprisings in territories that his father had conquered and the abandonment of numerous significant cities (primarily in Sumer).

High official of Samsu-iluna

When Hammurabi rose to prominence in Babylon, he was surrounded on all sides' by far more powerful rivals and only had authority over a tiny area in close proximity to the city. By the time of his death, he had taken control of

Mari, Assyria, Eshnunna, Sumer, and all of Mesopotamia. Elam and the Gutians had likewise been severely degraded and diminished by him.

These nations were crushed, but they were not completely destroyed; if Hammurabi had intended to join them to Babylon, he did not survive to see it through. Elam and Assyria exited Babylon's orbit a few years after his death, and uprisings had already begun in all of the conquered lands. Samsu-iluna was tasked with solving these problems and others. The monarch appeared to have won many battles despite his continuous campaigning, but he was powerless to avert the fall of the empire. Despite everything, he was able to maintain the foundation of his empire, which helped Babylon secure its place in history.

In the ninth year of Samsu-rule, iluna's a man going by the name Rim-sin (also known as Rim-sin II in the literature and possibly the nephew of the Rim-sin who opposed Hammurabi): started a rebellion against Babylonian rule in Larsa that quickly spread to 26 cities, including Uruk, Ur, Isin and Kisurra in the south, as well as Eshnunna.

Military advantage appears to have been held by Samsu-iluna. He handed the alliance a crushing blow within a year, removing the northern cities from the conflict. Iluni, the king of Eshnunna, was afterwards brought to Babylon and strangled to death. Samsu-army iluna's clashed with Rim-forces throughout the borders between Babylon, Sumer, and Elam during the course of the following four years. In the end, Samsu-iluna assaulted Ur, tore down its defences, and destroyed the city. He subsequently did the same to Uruk and Isin. The conflict was finally won by Rim-sin II and Larsa, who was ultimately vanquished.

A few years later, another pan-Sumerian uprising was started by an impostor going by the name of Ilum-ma-ili who claimed to be descended from the last king of Isin. Samsu-iluna led an army to Sumer, where they engaged in a conflict that ended in a draw. Ilum-ma-ili then won a further conflict, after which he established the First Dynasty of Sea-Land, which would rule over Sumer for the following 300 years. After this, Samsu-iluna appears to have adopted a defensive stance; in the 18th year of his reign, he oversaw the reconstruction of six strongholds near Nippur, which may have been done in an effort to maintain Babylonian sovereignty over that city. Ultimately, this was ineffective since Nippur had already acknowledged Ilum-ma-ili as king by the time Samsu-iluna passed away.

Eshnunna apparently had not accepted Babylonian rule either, since it again revolted in

Samsu-20th iluna's year. Samsu-iluna led his troops into the area and, perhaps after some slaughter, built the Dur-samsuiluna castle to control them. Later papers show Samsu-iluna adopting a more accommodative position toward rebuilding infrastructure and restoring rivers, therefore it appears that this was effective.

Elam and Assyria both reasserted their independence by taking advantage of the widespread anarchy. Samsu-raid iluna's on Uruk provided Kuturnahunte I of Elam with the chance he needed to invade the (now wall-less) city and loot it. One of the taken objects was an Inanna statue, which wasn't recovered until the reign of Ashurbanipal eleven centuries later. Asinum, a subordinate monarch of his fellow Amorite Hammurabi, was ousted from Assyria by a local vice regent named Puzur-Sin. Assyria had a period of civil strife after a local ruler named Ashur-dugul usurped the throne. A monarch by the name of Adasi eventually established a stable local dynasty in Assyria, eradicating any vestiges of Amorite-Babylonian influence, and Samsu-Iluna appears to have been helpless to intervene.

Samsu-iluna was eventually left with a kingdom that was barely any bigger than the one his father had started off with fifty years before (but which did leave him mastery of the Euphrates up to and including the ruins of Mari and its dependencies). Eshnunna's situation is unclear, and even while it may have remained in Babylonian hands, the city was worn out and its political power had faded.

It's possible that Samsu-expeditions iluna's weren't the only ones to damage Uruk and Ur, and his loss of Sumer may have been more of a strategic retreat than a defeat.

Record of sale of land in the era of King Samsu-iluna

After Samsu-tenth iluna's year in power, records in the cities of Ur and Uruk effectively come to an end, but its priests reportedly kept writing from further northern towns. Around this period, Larsa's records come to an end. Up to Samsu-29th iluna's year, records continue in Nippur and Isin until ending there as well. Archeological evidence indicates that these towns were mostly or entirely abandoned for hundreds of years, far into the Kassite period, during these gaps, which are also visible in the archaeological record.

Finding explanations for this is challenging. The incessant fighting couldn't have helped, but Samsu-iluna seems to have fought just as hard in the north, which was prosperous at the time. The development of Babylon signals the end of Sumerian cultural supremacy in Mesopotamia and the adoption of Akkadian as the language of the people and the government. It's possible that many who claimed cultural links to the Sumerian past relocated to the southern towns that Iluna-ilu ruled. Several members of his dynasty adopted Sumerian names, and it seems that they made a purposeful effort to reconnect with the Sumerian roots of the area. It is also conceivable that environmental or economic issues had a role. It is known that Hammurabi and Rim-sin implemented policies that affected the regional economy, and it is likely that they turned out to be unsustainable in the long run.

Chapter 7

King Abi-Eshuh

Abi-Eshuh, the eighth king of Babylon's First Dynasty, ruled for 28 years, from around 1648 to 1620 BC (short chronology) or 1711 to 1684 BC (middle chronology). Samsu-iluna, who was his father, came before him. His flamboyant titles were "king who makes the four quarters be at peace," "powerful monarch," "king of Babylon," "lord of the country of Sumer and Akkad," and "descendant of Sumu-la-El." His two vigorous military operations are likely what helped him do this. The fourth year of his name notes that he defeated the Kassite army.

He dammed the Tigris in an unsuccessful attempt to seize Ilum-ma-il, the founder of the Sealand Dynasty, according to The Chronicle of Early Kings. Because the events it recalls fall within three of his year-names, a clay cylinder fragment from Ki is speculatively attributed to him. The Tigris river is mentioned (year "o," the Tigris was dammed), as well as the Tigris gate (year "m," the ká-gal-i7idigna), the making of a mace for Marduk (year "g," and the digging of the Zubi canal (year "I,"). In the inscription of his son Ammi-Ditana and the genealogy of his descendant Amm-aduqa, he is referred to as "the mighty champion." Early in his reign, Kutir-nahhunte I, the king of the Elamites, led raids into Babylonia and devastated 30 towns.

Sea-land Dynasty

At Luaia, a settlement established by Ammu-Rpi on the Aratum Canal to the north of Babylon, two replicas of a building inscription memorialise his construction work. There is only one inscription, which can be read on an onyx eye stone honouring the goddess Ningal.

He is amply attested by the cylinder seal impressions of his servants, including Lamnum, son of Bl-kulla, Lutmar-Adad, son of Mr. Sipparim, Nabi'um-an[dasa], son of Ilu-ib[nu], son of Awl, Ilu-nir, son of Marduk-nir, a copy of Iddin-ama, sanga priest of the goddess Ninisina, Gimil-Gula and Taqis-Gula were the academics during the reign of Ab-eu, the king, according to the Uruk List of Kings and Sages.

Chapter 8

Neo-Assyrian Era

The Neo-Assyrian Empire was the fourth and last stage of ancient Assyrian history and the pinnacle of Assyria's existence as a sovereign nation. The Neo-Assyrian Empire, which began with the accession of Adad-nirari II in 911 BC, expanded to become the biggest empire in history by the time it dominated the ancient Near East for much of the 8th and 7th century BC.

Assyrian during Babylon war

Numerous academics consider the Neo-Assyrian Empire to be the first global empire in history due to its geopolitical hegemony and philosophy of global dominion. The empire reigned over all of Mesopotamia, the Levant, and Egypt, as well as parts of Anatolia, Arabia, modern-day Iran, and Armenia at its height, making it the most powerful military force in history. Since substantial sections of the previous Middle Assyrian Empire had been lost during a protracted period of decline, the early Neo-Assyrian rulers were primarily concerned with reestablishing Assyrian power over most of northern Mesopotamia and Syria. Assyria regained its position as the main force in the Near East under Ashurnasirpal II (reg. 883–859), who ruled the north unchallenged. Ashurnasirpal managed the move of the imperial capital from the old city of Assur to the more strategically positioned Nimrud. His wars extended as far as the Mediterranean.

Shalmaneser III, Ashurnasirpal II's successor (ruling from 859 to 824 BC), oversaw an even greater expansion of the empire, but his death brought in the so-called "era of the magnates," a time of stagnation. The main political power brokers at this period were well-known generals and bureaucrats, and central control was extremely lax. Tiglath-Pileser III (r. 745-727 BC), who restored Assyrian royal power and more than quadrupled the extent of the empire via extensive conquests, brought an end to this era. His most famous victories were the southern kingdom of Babylonia and a sizable portion of the Levant. Assyria reached its pinnacle under the rule of the Sargonid dynasty, which lasted from 722 BC until the fall of the empire.

The capital was moved to Nineveh by the Sargonid monarch Sennacherib (r. 705–681

BC), and under Esarhaddon (r. 681-669 BC), the kingdom attained its greatest size by conquering Egypt. Even though it was at the height of its strength, the Neo-Assyrian Empire fell quickly and violently in the late 7th century BC. This was due to a revolt by the Babylonians and an invasion by the Medes. Scholars continue to disagree on the reasons why Assyria may have fallen so swiftly.

The exceptional prosperity of the Neo-Assyrian Empire was made possible not only by Assyria's capacity for expansion but also—and probably more significantly—by its aptitude for successfully integrating conquered territories into its governing structure. The Neo-Assyrian Empire introduced several military, societal, and administrative improvements as the first empire of its size. Important military advancements were the widespread employment of cavalry and innovative siege warfare strategies. The Neo-Assyrian army pioneered tactics that would be employed in battle for millennia to come.

The Neo-Assyrian Empire created a complex state communication system combining relay stations and well-kept roadways to address the difficulty of communicating across great distances. It took until the 19th century AD for the Middle East to catch up to the Neo-Assyrian Empire in terms of the pace of official dispatches. The Neo-Assyrian Empire also employed a strategy of resettlement, wherein certain residents from conquered territories were sent to the Assyrian core and to undeveloped regions.The Neo-Assyrian Empire left behind a rich cultural legacy. The Neo-Assyrian Empire's political structures served as a template for the empires that came after it, and the Neo-Assyrian kings' doctrine of universal rule stimulated, via the idea of translatio imperii, the same notions of claims to global dominance in later empires as late as the early modern era. Through the succeeding post-imperial era and beyond, the Neo-Assyrian Empire had a significant role in later northern Mesopotamian folklore and literary traditions.

The Neo-Assyrian era had a significant impact on Judaism, which in turn had an impact on Christianity and Islam. Numerous Biblical stories appear to have been influenced by previous Assyrian mythology and history, and early Jewish theology was greatly influenced by Neo-Assyrian thought. The Neo-Assyrian Empire is well known today for the alleged extreme cruelty of the Neo-Assyrian army, yet the Assyrians weren't particularly violent compared to other civilizations of the period or to civilizations throughout human history. Prior to the establishment of the Neo-Assyrian Empire, imperialism and the desire to create a global, all-encompassing empire were well-established elements of royal philosophy in the ancient Near East. The rulers of the many Mesopotamian city-states—the most notable of which were Ur, Uruk, Lagash, Umma, and Kish—fought among themselves often throughout the Early Dynastic Period (c. 2900–2350 BC) in order to build miniature hegemonic empires and to gain an advantage over the other city-states. These little disputes eventually grew into a widespread desire for universal control.

Because Mesopotamia was seen to correlate to the entire world at this early time, achieving a position of global dominance was not viewed as an entirely unattainable endeavour. Lugalzaggesi, king of Uruk, who unified all of Lower Mesopotamia in the 24th century BC, was one of the early Mesopotamian "world conquerors." The Akkadian Empire, founded by Sargon of Akkad in 2334 BC, is widely recognised as the first significant Mesopotamian Empire.

After the Akkadian Empire, a great number of imperialist nations arose and disappeared in Mesopotamia and the rest of the Near East. The majority of early empires and kingdoms, like the Akkadian Empire, were confined to a small number of core provinces, and the majority of their people only loosely acknowledged the rule of the central government. Nevertheless, the goal for world dominance permeated

Mesopotamian monarchs' royal ideas for thousands of years. This trend was aided by the memory of the Akkadian Empire and was embodied by titles like "king of the Universe" or "king of the Four Corners of the World."

The kings of Assyria, who ruled in what had been been the northern region of the Akkadian Empire, likewise displayed this ambition. With the emergence of the Middle Assyrian Empire in the 14th century BC, Assyria, which had previously only existed as a city-state centred on the city of Assur, entered its first period of supremacy. Assyria rose to prominence during the reign of the Assyrian monarch Adad-nirari-I (r. c. 1305–1274 BC) and under Tukulti-Ninurta-I (r. c. 1243–1207 BC), the kingdom attained its greatest size and became the dominating force in Mesopotamia, briefly subjugating Babylonia in the south.Following Tukulti-murder, Ninurta's the Middle Assyrian Empire had a protracted period of collapse and was eventually confined to simply the Assyrian heartland. Although Tiglath-Pileser I (r. 1114–1076 BC), who once again increased Assyrian power, halted this era of decline, his conquests overstretched Assyria and could not be sustained by his successors. Only under the rule of Ashur-dan II (r. 934–912 BC), the final Middle Assyrian monarch, who conducted campaigns in the northeast and northwest, was the trend of decline somewhat reversible.

Chapter 9

Rise of Assyrian Power

Babylonia was continuously ruled or directly ruled by the Assyrians during the reign of the Neo-Assyrian Empire (916–609 BC). Babylonia was in a permanent state of uprising under Sennacherib of Assyria. It was led by a leader named Merodach-Baladan, who was allied with the Elamites, and was only put an end to by the whole destruction of the city of Babylon. Its walls, temples, and palaces were demolished in 689 BC, and the debris was dumped into the Arakhtu, the sea that bordered the older Babylon on the southern side. Many people were appalled by the destruction of the holy complex, and Sennacherib's subsequent killing by two of his own sons while they prayed to the deity Nisroch was seen as a gesture of atonement.

Esarhaddon, his successor, raced to reconstruct the ancient city as a result, and he now spends a portion of the year there. After his passing, his eldest son, the Assyrian ruler Shamash-shum-ukin, who later initiated a civil war against his own brother, Ashurbanipal, who ruled in Nineveh, was in charge of Babylonia. In order to fight Assyria, Shamash-shum-ukin solicited the aid of several other nations, including Elam, Persia, the Chaldeans and Suteans of southern

Mesopotamia, as well as the Canaanites and Arabs who lived in the southern Mesopotamian deserts.

The early Neo-Assyrian rulers fought to stop the long period of Assyrian collapse and regain the former domains of their kingdom via decades of military victories. The early Neo-Assyrian kings are thought to have primarily sought to restore Assyria's position at the height of the Middle Assyrian Empire. Although the Neo-Assyrian Empire has occasionally in the past been considered a completely new phenomenon only loosely connected to earlier Assyrian history, it is now considered more probable due to evidence from royal inscriptions and the nature and extent of the campaigns undertaken.

The fact that the two dynasties' rulers are descended from the same extended family should further debunk any impression that they are separate entities. Another justification for expansion was to portray the campaigns as liberation wars intended to free Assyrians who no longer resided in Assyrian territory from their new foreign rulers; tangible evidence from a number of sites retaken under the early Neo-Assyrian Empire shows that Assyrian culture survived outside of Assyrian borders during the Middle Assyrian Empire's decline.

The area up to the Khabur River in the west was primarily the focus of the early Neo-Assyrian efforts at reconquest. Ashur-dan II made Katmuu in this area one of his first victories, but rather than annexing it completely, he made it a vassal state. This implies that the early Neo-Assyrian monarchs had very few resources at their disposal and that the imperial reconquista project had to start almost from scratch. The early Neo-Assyrian monarchs' effective expansion was a remarkable accomplishment in this era.

The slow start of this project was witnessed during the initial phase of the Assyrian reconquista, which spanned the reigns of the first two Neo-Assyrian kings, Adad-nirari II (r. 911-891 BC) and Tukulti-Ninurta II (r. 890-884 BC), and began under Ashur-dan II near the end of the Middle Assyrian period. The majority of Ashur-efforts Dan's were successful in laying the groundwork for the longer-term work done by Tukulti-Ninurta and Adad-nirari. The conflicts fought to the southeast, past the Little Zab River, were among the conquests of Adad-nirari, and they were the most crucial from a strategic perspective. These territories had previously been governed by the Babylonians. The Assyrian army travelled during one of Adad-campaigns nirari's as far south as Der, which is near to the frontier of the western kingdom of Elam. Adad-nirari secured the city of Arrapha, despite his failure to conquer lands that were so distant from the Assyrian core (modern-day Kirkuk). Later on, more Assyrian operations into regions in the east were launched from Arrapha. The fact that Adad-nirari was able to negotiate a boundary arrangement with the Babylonian king Nabu-shuma-ukin I (r. 900–887 BC), sealed by their each marriage to a daughter of the other, and is a monument to his might. In the west, Adad-nirari carried on Ashur-work; dan's throughout his battles, he subdued several minor kingdoms. Several tiny nations were turned into vassals, like Guzana, while others, like Nisibis, were placed under puppet rulers who supported Assyria.

Adad-nirari was able to collect tribute from all the regional kings on a protracted march down the Khabur and Euphrates rivers after his victorious campaigns in the area without encountering any military resistance. In addition to his wars, he also oversaw significant construction projects; the city of Apku, which was devastated circa 1000 BC and was situated between Nineveh and Sinjar, was restored and turned into a significant administrative hub.

Tukulti-Ninurta, the son of Adad-nirari, carried on his father's policies even though his rule was brief. Tukulti-Ninurta carried out his father's march through the Euphrates and Khabur in 885 BC, but he did it in the other way, starting in Dur-Kurigalzu and moving north while collecting tribute. During this march, some of the southern cities gave tribute to Tukulti-Ninurta were traditionally more allied with Babylon. Tukulti-Ninurta also engaged in armed conflict with minor nations in the east in an effort to bolster Assyrian rule in that region. He conquered several nations, including Kirruri, Hubushkia, and Gilzanu. Gilzanu frequently provided Assyria with horses in later times.

Chapter 10

King Ashurnasirpal

Ashurnasirpal II, the son and successor of Tukulti-Ninurta (883–859 BC), began the second stage of the Assyrian reconquista. Although it would not yet acquire dominance similar to that under its whole domination in following centuries, Assyria rose to become the dominating political force in the Near East during his administration. Ashurnasirpal had a complicated nature; he was a ruthless warrior and one of the most terrible kings in Assyrian history, yet he also cared about the people, seeking to improve their well-being and comfort and being noted for building huge water and food depots in case of need. Ashurnasirpal received an astonishing amount of resources with which he could strive to re-establish Assyrian control as a consequence of the victorious conquests of his forebears. The rebellious cities of Suru and Tela were the targets of Ashurnasirpal's first campaign, which took place in 883 BC along the northern bank of the Tigris River. He mercilessly suppressed the populace of Tela by, among other penalties, amputating fingers, limbs, noses, ears, and eyes, as well as approving impalements and decapitations.

King Ashurnasirpal

In his final battles, Ashurnasirpal engaged in three wars with the kingdom of Zamua in the eastern Zagros Mountains, many conflicts with the northern kingdoms of Nairi and Urartu, and, most noticeably, nearly constant warfare with the Aramean and Neo-Hittite kingdoms in the west. By the time of Ashurnasirpal's accession to the throne, the Arameans and Neo-Hittites had developed into sophisticated kingdoms, presumably in reaction to Assyrian pressure. The Aramean monarch Ahuni, who was in charge of the town or area of Bit Adini, was one of Ashurnasirpal's most tenacious adversaries. After years of fighting, Ahuni finally recognised Ashurnasirpal as his suzerain after his soldiers repeatedly crossed the Khabur and Euphrates.

Ahuni's defeat was crucial because it gave Assyrian armies their first chance to conduct a campaign farther west than the Euphrates since Ashur-bel-kala (r. 1073–1056 BC), two centuries earlier. Ashurnasirpal took advantage of this chance. He marched to Lebanon and subsequently to the Mediterranean Sea coast during his tenth expedition. Many countries on the route, notably Carchemish and Patina as well as Phoenician cities like Sidon, Byblos, Tyre, and Arwad, paid homage to Ashurnasirpal to avoid being invaded, even though few of them at this stage were legally absorbed into the empire. According to Ashurnasirpal's royal inscriptions, he and his soldiers ceremonially cleansed their weapons in the Mediterranean.

Assur, which is still the imperial center of religion, was reduced to becoming a mainly ceremonial city after the creation of the new capital. Ashurnasirpal also built a zoo, which is thought to be the first significant zoo ever built, as well as colossal city walls that were 7.5 kilometers (4.6 miles) long, palaces, temples, royal offices, and various residential buildings. These botanical gardens were filled with exotic plants that he brought back from his extensive campaigns. The inscriptions of Ashurnasirpal don't explain why the capital was changed. Modern scholars have suggested a number of explanations, such as the possibility that he lost interest in Assur because there wasn't much space left in the ancient capital to make a mark, Nimrud's significant role in terms of regional trade networks, and Nimrud's more central location within the empire.

Ashurnasirpal hosted a lavish celebration to mark the end of his construction work in Nimrud in 864 BC. This event, which was attended by 69,574 people over the course of ten days and included 16,000 citizens of the new capital and 5,000 foreign dignitaries, has been dubbed by some scholars as the greatest party in history. In addition to innumerable other goods, Ashurnasirpal's inscriptions include 10,000 birds, 10,000 jugs of beer, and 10,000 skins of wine among the food and drink consumed.

King Shalmaneser meeting with King of Babylon

Shalmaneser III, who ruled from 859 to 824 BC, carried on his father Ashurnasirpal's strong military policies and significantly increased Assyrian territory. During Shalmaneser's rule, Assyrian authority was strengthened over the western regions bordering the Khabur and Euphrates rivers. Ahuni of Bit Adini withstood Shalmaneser for a number of years until giving up to him in the winter of 857/856 BC. The city was renamed Kar-Salmanuaared ("fortress of Shalmaneser") when Shalmaneser visited it in the summer of the following year. He also made it the administrative headquarters of a new province that was put under the turtanu (commander in chief). Shalmaneser appointed other strong men, or "magnates," in command of other imperially weak provinces and territories.

At this time, Urartu in the north was Assyria's most formidable and dangerous adversary. Urartu closely followed Assyria's administrative structure, culture, writing system, and religious beliefs. Similar to the Assyrian rulers in many ways, the Urartian monarchs were autocrats as well. The Assyrians were likewise influenced by Urartu.

Shalmaneser may have drawn inspiration from Urartu encounters for Assyrian irrigation technologies and cavalry troops, for example. Even though the Taurus Mountains separated Urartu and Assyria, the monarchs of both nations engaged in imperialist expansionism, which frequently resulted in military confrontations. One of Shalmaneser's most daring military operations in Assyrian history took place in 856 BC, when he marched over steep terrain to the Euphrates's source before striking Urartu from the west. Shalmaneser's army destroyed the Urartian heartland, sacked the Urartian city of Arzashkun, marched into what is now western Iran, and then returned to Arbela in Assyria, forcing the Urartian king Arame to escape.

Shalmaneser was unable to take full advantage of the circumstances, despite the fact that his successful battle against Urartu forced many of the petty nations in northern Syria to pay homage to him. At Tell Qarqur in Syria in 853 BC, a vast coalition of western nations came together to collaborate against Assyrian expansion. Hadadezer, the king of Aram-Damascus, commanded a coalition that comprised several monarchs of other nations, including the earliest historically documented Israel and Arab sultans.

The coalition was fought against by Shalmaneser the same year it was established. Although Assyrian chronicles state that he won the ensuing War of Qarqar, it is more likely that no significant political or territorial gains were made, making the battle more likely to have been a draw. Following Qarqar, Shalmaneser concentrated heavily on the south and, in 851–850 BC, helped Marduk-zakir-shumi I of Babylon put down a rebellion led by his brother Marduk-bel–ushati. After disposing of the insurgent, Shalmaneser spent some time touring Babylonian cities and aiding Marduk-zakir-shumi by battling the Chaldeans in the far south of Mesopotamia.

Assyria had a strong appreciation for Babylonian culture, and Shalmaneser was proud of his partnership with the latter. A renowned piece of surviving art depicts the two kings shaking hands. After the alliance against him disintegrated with Hadadezer's death in 841 BC, Shalmaneser waged another expedition in Syria in the 840s and 830s BC and was successful in collecting tribute from several western kingdoms. Three times, Assyrian armies attempted to take Damascus proper, but they failed. Shalmaneser's vigorous operations rapidly overextended the empire, which led to his unsuccessful attempts to properly establish Assyrian dominance in Syria. Shalmaneser's soldiers crossed into Cilicia in Anatolia in the 830s BC, and in 836 BC, he arrived at ubuna (near present-day Ereli), one of the westernmost points ever attained by Assyrian forces. Despite the fact that Shalmaneser conquered a large area and caused dread among the other kings of the Near East, he lacked the resources to consolidate and establish his new domains, and imperial power remained fragile in many regions.

Chapter 11

The fall of Babylon Empire

Babylonian cuneiform name for Nabonidus is "Nabonidus in Akkadian." The final monarch of the Neo-Babylonian Empire, Nabû-naid (meaning "May Nabu be glorified" or "Nabu is honoured"), ruled from 556 BC until Babylon fell to Cyrus the Great's Achaemenid Empire in 539 BC. Thousands of years of Sumero-Akkadian states, kingdoms, and empires came to an end with the reign of Nabonidus, the last native monarch of ancient Mesopotamia.

Graynite stele of Nabonidus

Nabonidus was one of the most dynamic and individualistic kings of his period. He is known as the last independent king of Babylon, and some academics have described him as the first archaeologist and an unconventional religious reformer. Given that Nabonidus made no genealogical claims to family with other kings, it is unknown where he came from, how he became connected to past monarchy, and what claim he had to the throne. Although he is known to have had a notable career of some type before he became king, this shows that he was not linked to or connected to the Chaldean line of Babylonian kings. He could have been related to the Chaldean monarchs by a marriage, probably to a Nebuchadnezzar II (reigned 605–562 BC) daughter.

Adad-guppi, the mother of Nabonidus, was of Assyrian or Aramean descent. Little is known about his father, Nabu-balatsu-iqbi, although it's assumed that he was either Assyrian or Aramean. According to some historians, either Adad-guppi or Nabu-balatsu-iqbi belonged to the Sargonid dynasty, which ruled the Neo-Assyrian Empire until its collapse in 609 BC.

Following the deposition and death of Labashi-Marduk (r. 556 BC) in a scheme that was probably directed by Nabonidus's son Belshazzar, Nabonidus was, to his own apparent astonishment, crowned king. Inscriptions and other sources indicate that Nabonidus attempted to elevate the moon god Sîn and lower the prominence of Marduk, the ancient national god of Babylon, during his rule. The extent to which Nabonidus' dedication to Sîn led to religious reforms is debatable, despite some claims that he wanted to totally replace Marduk with Sîn as the leader of the Mesopotamian pantheon. Nabonidus lived in self-imposed exile in Tayma, Arabia, from 552 BC to 543/542 BC for unspecified reasons, presumably because of conflicts with the Babylonian oligarchs and church. Belshazzar served as Babylonia's regent during this time, but Nabonidus was still acknowledged as the country's ruler.

Nabonidus intensified his religious activities after his return to Babylonia in 543/542 BC and restored the Ekhulkhul, the temple devoted to Sîn in the important northern city of Harran. Nabonidus' rule came to a sudden end when Cyrus the Great swiftly overcame his empire in 539 BC. Following the decisive battle of Opis, the Persians marched amiably into Babylon. Several versions claim that Belshazzar was murdered, but Nabonidus was kidnapped and spared, probably permitted to travel to the Carmanian area. Even during the reign of Darius the Great (r. 522-486 BC), Nabonidus may still have been living in exile.

In his inscriptions, Nabonidus describes his father, Nabu-balatsu-iqbi, as a "knowing counsellor," "intelligent prince," "perfect prince," and "heroic governor. "It is generally believed that Nabonidus was not directly associated with Babylonia's governing dynasty because Nabu-balatsu-iqbi is not tied to any Babylonian monarch in his inscriptions (the Chaldean dynasty). Nabonidus does not claim to be descended from any of the rulers of Babylon mentioned in his inscriptions, though he does allude to them as such. Nabonidus makes no reference of his father's ancestry or ethnicity in any of the inscriptions; all that is said about him is that he was valiant, clever, and pious. Curiously, Nabonidus' father's rank and position are unknown since no one with the name Nabu-balatsu-iqbi who can be properly recognised as Nabonidus' father occurs in records previous to Nabonidus' reign. Nabonidus's inscriptions frequently allude to Nabu-balatsu-iqbi as "prince," which shows that he had a high position and was significant politically.

Adad-guppi, Nabonidus' mother, was born in 648 or 649 BC. There is no proof that Adad-guppi was the concubine of Nabonidus' forebears, despite the fact that she was originally thought to have been a member of the Babylonian royal harem. Although her inscriptions say she had influence with the monarchs Nabopolassar (reigned 626–605 BC), Nebuchadnezzar II (reigned 605–562 BC), and Neriglissar (reigned 560–556 BC), she was nevertheless important in the royal Babylonian court. Although there is no solid proof, Adad-guppi is frequently believed to have originated from the important city of Harran in northern Mesopotamia (where she subsequently lived) and to have Assyrian descent.

Paul-Alain Beaulieu claims that the only way to account for Nabonidus' subsequent, obsessive interest in Harran, a little city in his empire, is if he and his mother were born there. The Dynastic Prophecy, a later work published centuries after Alexander the Great conquered Babylonia, supports the idea that Nabonidus would have come from Harran since it identifies Nabonidus as the founder and sole representative of the "dynasty of Harran." Adagoppe may have been Aramean rather than Assyrian, according to Beaulieu, as her name "looks to be Aramean." Adad-guppi was a priestess of Sîn, the moon deity, at Harran. The only titles Adad-guppi claims in her inscriptions are "mother of Nabonidus" and "worshipper of Sîn, Ningal, Nusku, and Sadarnunna," therefore there is no proof that she had a prominent position among priestesses.

Nabu-balatsu-iqbi was undoubtedly also a well-known inhabitant of that city, maybe of Assyrian or Aramean ancestry, given Adad-affiliation guppi's with Harran and the likelihood that she had married him young (as was customary in ancient Mesopotamia). Jamie Novotny and Frauke Weiershäuser hypothesised that Nabu-balatsu-iqbi could have been an Aramaean king. There is no proof to support Stephen Herbert Langdon's theory that Nabu-balatsu-iqbi was an Ashurbanipal's brother and the son of Esarhaddon (r. 681-669 BC).

It is likely that Nabonidus was an only child based on his own inscriptions and those of Adad-guppi, in which he is often referred to as her "only son." Adagoppe most likely arrived in Babylon for the first time as a prisoner after the Babylonians and Medes took Harran in 610 BC as part of their invasion of the Assyrian Empire. She had reached the age of 39 by 610 BC. Nabonidus, whose birth year is unknown, was presumably already born at this point. Adagoppe asserts in one of her inscriptions that she witnessed four generations of her descendants throughout her lifetime, including her great-great-grandchildren (i.e., Nabonidus's great-grandchildren). Nabonidus cannot have been born later than c. 615 BC, while he very well may have been born earlier. If the interval between generations is believed to be around 20 to 25 years, and presuming her great-great-grandchildren were around five years old when Adagoppe's death.

Nabonidus could have been wed to one of Nebuchadnezzar II's daughters, a union that might have been facilitated by his mother's power. Being related to the royal dynasty would help to explain Nabonidus' ascent to the throne, as well as subsequent historical traditions that refer to Nabonidus' son Belshazzar as Nebuchadnezzar II's descendent. Nebuchadnezzar II's (grand) son Belshazzar is alluded to in the Hebrew Bible's Book of Daniel.

The assertion that Belshazzar was a descendant of Nebuchadnezzar II could really have originated from royal propaganda rather than accurate genealogical data. Nitocris is referred to as the "final great queen" of the Babylonian Empire by the ancient Greek historian Herodotus, despite the fact that neither that name nor any others are found in texts from modern-day Babylonia. Although William H. Shea suggested in 1982 that Nitocris may be tentatively identified as the name of Nabonidus's wife and Belshazzar's mother, Herodotus' description of Nitocris contains a wealth of legendary material that makes it difficult to determine whether he uses the name to refer to Nabonidus's wife or mother.

Adad-guppi also asserted in her inscriptions that Nabonidus belonged to the dynastic dynasty of Ashurbanipal, monarch of the Neo-Assyrian Empire (669–631 BC). Adad-guppi was born in Ashurbanipal's 20th year as king, per her inscriptions.

Chapter 12

Throne of Nabonidus

Herodotus claims that an official by the name of Labynetus (also known as Nabonidus in ancient Greek sources) attended the discussions between the Median and Lydian empires in 585 BC following the Battle of the Eclipse as a mediator and witness on behalf of Babylon. It's probable that the Nabonidus who subsequently rose to power in Babylon was this diplomat.

Nabonidus Stele

Following the dissolution of the Chaldean dynasty's direct dynastic line, Nabonidus ascension to the throne occurred. The kingdom was inherited by Neriglissar's son Labashi-Marduk in April 556 BC following the brief rule of Neriglissar, a son-in-law of Nebuchadnezzar II. Berossus falsely claimed that Labashi-Marduk ruled for nine months (although this may be due to a scribal error) and said that because of his "evil ways," Labashi-companions

Marduk's plotted to have him killed, and that's how the "kid king" was put to death. The conspirators then decided that one of them, Nabonnedos (Nabonidus), should govern. Unknown factors may have led to the coup against Labashi-Marduk.

Despite Labashi-riches Marduk's father and connections, it's probable that they were still viewed as commoners who lacked aristocratic lineage. It is conceivable that Labashi-Marduk was the son of Neriglissar and a different bride, but it is also plausible that he was the grandson of Nebuchadnezzar II through his mother, making him a member of the royal dynasty. Thus, Labashi-accession Marduk's to the throne may have represented a real end to the Nebuchadnezzar II dynasty and as such, might have sparked rebellion among the Babylonian people. Berossus refers to Labashi-Marduk as a kid, but as commercial documents from two years earlier show that Labashi-Marduk was managing his own affairs at that time, it's plausible that he became king as an adult.

Although Nabonidus says in his inscriptions that he had few followers and that he did not desire the throne himself, he must have played a key role in the plot that resulted in Labashi-ouster Marduk's and execution. Throughout his reign, Nabonidus had the backing of the Babylonian military, and it's conceivable that the army had a hand in his ascent to the throne. Despite Berossus's assertion that Labashi-Marduk ruled for nine months, the Uruk King List only records his reign as lasting three months, and contract tablets from Babylonia imply that he may have had a two-month maximum reign.

It seems that there was either a time of disarray following a covert palace takeover or a brief civil war. According to contract tablets, Labashi-Marduk was still regarded as king in the cities of Sippar and Uruk until at least 19 June. The 26 June tablet at Sippar is the earliest one dating to Nabonidus' reign. However, a tablet from Nippur that was inscribed as early as May 25 is dated to Nabonidus' reign, while the latest tablet from Babylon that is attributed to Labashi-reign Marduk's is from May 24. The earliest tablet from Babylon proper that is dated to Nabonidus is from July 14. This evidence may be explained by proposing that Labashi-Marduk was still recognised as king in certain outlying cities until June, despite the fact that Nabonidus may have been recognised as monarch in the Babylonian heartland, including Nippur and Babylon, as early as May 25. Nabonidus-dated tablets from all around Babylonia are known by the end of June 556 BC.

It is thus probable that, despite the fact that Nabonidus was a key player in the conspiracy that overthrew Labashi-Marduk and killed him, he had no intention of ascending to the throne himself but was persuaded to do so by the other conspirators. Belshazzar, the son of Nabonidus, is likely the main planner behind the plot against Labashi-Marduk. As the chosen heir to the throne and the recipient of the vast private estates of Labashi-Marduk, Belshazzar was the main benefactor of the entire situation. Overnight, he rose to become one of the richest and most powerful people in Babylonia. Belshazzar believed that by installing his father on the throne as an elderly man (implying that his reign could be expected to be transitory, lasting only a few years), he had secured the throne for himself in the future. However, Belshazzar could not have claimed the throne for himself while his father was still alive.

Nabonidus' first official act as king was a visit to the city of Sippar on July 4, 556 BC, when he gave three minas of gold to the Ebabbar temple, the city's temple. Given that Sippar had only recognised Labashi-Marduk as king two weeks earlier, about a month after Nabonidus had been crowned, the visit may have had a political motive. Nabonidus led the Babylonian army on an expedition to Hume, eastern Cilicia, where Neriglissar had campaigned in 557 BC, in the fall of 556 BC. The fact that Nabonidus launched his expedition there so soon after Neriglissar's campaign may indicate that Nabonidus was worried about the security of the empire in general or that Syria, which was ruled by the Bablyonians, was in danger from Cilician raiders. As a result of the original campaign's success, Babylon received captives, presents, and loot for use in the yearly New Year's festival. According to Babylonian archives, 2,850 captives were eventually given away as slaves to the temple.

Nabonidus travelled briefly to southern Babylonia after the New Year's festivities to visit the towns of Kish, Larsa, Uruk, and Ur. He carried out thorough renovations at Uruk's Eanna temple, changing the sacrificial offering schedule, and bringing back several sacrifices that had been suspended under Neriglissar's rule. A fragmentary record shows that Nabonidus launched a second successful campaign to Cilicia in 555 BC, possibly destroying the Syrian city of Hama along the route.

Although Nabonidus made the customary royal contributions to the Babylonian temples, the main construction project of his reign, which was announced as his intention shortly after he was crowned, was rebuilding the Harran temple Ekhulkhul, which was dedicated to Sîn and had been destroyed by the Medes in 610 BC. The demolition of the temple occurred precisely 54 years before Nabonidus became king, which he saw as a remarkable coincidence at the start of his rule. Three cycles of 18 years each, or 54 years, make up a full lunar cycle.

Even while restoration work on the Elhulkhul did not begin until Nabonidus returned from a protracted trip in Tayma in Arabia, it is probable that it began much earlier because it seems to have been his ambition ever since he ascended to the king. The Medes endangered Harran by "surrounding" it, according to Nabonidus' inscriptions, and it's conceivable that the prospect of Median invaders hindering construction efforts caused construction to be put off until later in his reign. According to his inscriptions, Marduk and Sîn both gave Nabonidus the instruction to rebuild the temple in a dream. The gods also promised him that the Medes would ultimately be restored, allowing building to start without worrying about attacks.

Nabonidus may have had political motivations for restoring the Ekhulkhul and the city of Harran that surrounded it in addition to his personal religious convictions. Political hegemony in the Near East had been split between Babylonia and the Medes since the collapse of Assyria, a problem that had not been addressed by the reign of Nabonidus. It appears that Nabonidus was getting ready to settle the issue since he frequently compares himself to his conqueror and warrior ancestors

Nebuchadnezzar II and Neriglissar, and because various inscriptions mention his being busy with military concerns in the year of his accession.

Chapter 13
Nabonidus Religious Policies

Nabonidus worshiping moon and sun

Nabonidus is often portrayed as trying to change religion in Babylonia by elevating the moon god Sîn to the position of supreme deity and debasing Marduk, the nation's patron deity. Sîn's elevation was comparable to the elevation of Inanna to a prominent location in Uruk during the Akkadian Empire, more than a thousand years earlier, or the initial elevation of Marduk in Babylonia during the reign of Nebuchadnezzar I (r. c. 1125–1104 BC). The endeavour to exalt Sîn failed in contrast to these past successful exaltations.

This failure can be attributed to the fact that Sîn's exaltation encountered significant internal opposition in Babylonia and that the Persian invasion and conquest ended the political channels through which the exaltation could be carried out. The Verse Account of Nabonidus relates to attempts to elevate Sîn to the top position in the Mesopotamian pantheon in addition to erecting inscriptions. Other Nabonidus-related inscriptions and records began to get scholarly attention after the Verse Account was published in 1924. Notably, several of his inscriptions either completely exclude Marduk as the head of the pantheon or fail to mention him at all, and they frequently lavish excessive adulation on Sîn.

Given the wide variations in the epithets applied to Marduk and Sîn over his reign, it is likely that Nabonidus' devotion to Sîn grew during the course of his rule. Even at the beginning of his rule, Marduk was only given the bare minimum of titles, including "king of the gods," "lord of lords," and "leader of the gods," which is far less than is typical. Sîn, on the other hand, receives a wide variety of epithets, some of which are novel. Some examples are "shining deity," "light of mankind," "exalted god," and "exalted lord." Early in his rule, Nabonidus could scarcely have moved to enact religious changes, especially given that he had just usurped the throne. His earliest inscriptions appear to be conventional on the surface, but they indicate deliberate restraint in the exaltation of Marduk and deliberate exaggerated glorification of Sîn.

Inscriptions from the period Nabonidus spent in Tayma seem to indicate that the king returned to "orthodoxy" during this time. Inscriptions no longer exalt Sîn to an excessive degree (the deity is barely mentioned), and instead give Marduk more elaborate and appropriate epithets, such as "foremost of the gods," "lofty king of the gods," "lord of everything," and "king of heaven and the underworld." These inscriptions contrast sharply with those written by Nabonidus in the years after his return to Babylon, where Sîn is frequently extolled and Marduk is largely neglected, with the exception of one inscription in which he just serves as Sîn's companion. It is probable that the return to orthodoxy occurred when Nabonidus was in Tayma since Belshazzar was in charge of Babylonia at the time. Belshazzar may have persuaded Nabonidus to leave Babylonia and introduced a definite return to orthodoxy out of fear of conflict with the oligarchs and clergy.

Inscriptions that ascribe Nebuchadnezzar's victories to Sîn rather than Marduk or the Assyrian god Ashur and one that claims Sîn, rather than the Assyrian monarchs Esarhaddon and Ashurbanipal, gave Sîn the authority to govern the entire world are examples of historical revisionism. Sîn also took over Marduk's function of announcing candidates for kingship. According to one inscription,

Nabonidus was predestined for the throne by the gods Sîn and Ningal (Sîn's consort) while still within his mother. After the Ekhulkhul was rebuilt, Sîn's exaltation peaked, and the most recent religious book we have from Nabonidus even refers to the temples of Esagila and Ezida in Babylon, where Marduk had his original residences, as Sîn's temples and houses. Although it does not appear that Sîn ever "usurped" the Esagila, Nabonidus seriously considered having Sîn replace Marduk in the temple. Nabonidus supported this by pointing out that the temple contained lunar symbolism because it was marked with a crescent symbol, indicating that Sîn was its intended original owner. The greatest known appellation ever offered to a Mesopotamian deity, "god of gods," is bestowed upon Sîn in one inscription.

There is not much tangible proof for Nabonidus's religious convictions, and there are no theoretical underpinnings for the king's religion and beliefs in any of the writings that have survived. The idea that Nabonidus was a religious reformer is not held by all historians. Nabonidus "did not want to create any unique role for [Sîn] in Babylon," claims Donald Wiseman. As with all previous Babylonian monarchs, Wiseman describes Nabonidus as being intensely religious and in favour of Marduk. Nabonidus is also mentioned in inscriptions as having restored temples in

Larsa, Sippar, Nippur, the Elhulkhul temple, and Babylon itself.

Wiseman says that the king's introduction of a new royal cash box in temples and sanctuaries, wherein some of the temples' income was to be provided to the king under the supervision of royal officials, is what caused the opposition by religious officials to Nabonidus. He also notes that Cyrus the Great's later documents portraying Nabonidus as irreverent in regards to Marduk may be propaganda. Weiherhäuser and Novotny noted that while Nabonidus frequently utilises very high epithets for Sîn, the majority of them are typically restricted to inscriptions and manuscripts that detail construction on the Ekhulkhul temple at Harran, Sîn's cultic centre. Weiherhäuser and Novotny conclude that the evidence is insufficient to prove that Nabonidus fervently advocated Sîn and aspired to completely replace Marduk inside Babylonia.

Chapter 14

Babylon in Crises

Nabonidus left Tayma and came back to Babylon for an unknown reason. Possible theories include dread of Cyrus the Great's rising power or even significant differences with Belshazzar over religion and the scope of his rule. After his return, he quickly started to put his desired religious changes into practise. He may have put out so much effort because of his old age and desire to see the reforms through before his passing.

The primary undertaking under Nabonidus' latter rule was the completion of the construction work at the Ekhulkhul in Harran, with the temple being reconstructed on top of its original foundation. According to Nabonidus, the restoration of the temple was his most significant accomplishment. Construction projects were also carried out in Ur, Larsa, Sippar, and Akkad. According to some evidence, Babylonia had a famine under Nabonidus' latter rule. The fact that the public did not accept the king's religious changes appears to have been attributed by Nabonidus to Sîn's fury, whilst the populace likely attributed it to Marduk's wrath due to the king's heretical beliefs.

King Cyrus

The New Year's festival, which had been postponed while the monarch was away in Tayma, was once more observed yearly following Nabonidus's return. Given that the festival served as an annual restoration of Marduk's sovereignty and was held to secure Babylon's prosperity, it is interesting that it was stopped while Nabonidus was away. Cyrus' menace become more imminent. It appears that there was already a conflict between Persian and Babylonian forces in the winter of 540/539 BC, close to Uruk, though the records are too few to say with confidence.

This shows that Nabonidus anticipated a Persian invasion and began laying the groundwork months in advance. Although transporting sculptures in this way created a great deal of disruption in the cults of the gods moved, it was the customary way to protect the divine statues in times of war (victorious enemy often took cultic statues). For instance, in order to prevent the cult from being disrupted, it is likely that offerings of food and drink had to be transported from Uruk to Babylon in order to be given to the statue when it was transported from Uruk to Babylon.

The deities of certain nearby cities, like Cutha, Sippar, and Borsippa, were not transported to the capital. Although the cause of this is unknown, several ideas have been put forth. The Nabonidus Cylinder's translator, Sidney Smith, proposed in 1924 that Nabonidus might have also called the statues of other cities to the capital, but that the local priesthoods rejected him because they disapproved of his attempt at reshaping religion. The Median Wall, which was constructed under Nebuchadnezzar II to defend against attacks from the north, and strong fortifications in the Babylonian heartland of Sippar, Borsippa, and Cutha prevented these cities from needing to send their statues to Babylon for protection, whereas less well-defended cities like Uruk did. This alternative hypothesis was later put forth by Smith. Given that Kish and Khursagkalamma were closer to Babylon than Sippar was, this seems improbable. Additionally, Stefan Zawadzki showed in 2012 that Sippar did transfer certain gods to Babylon, but not their primary statue of their patron deity Shamash. The reason Sippar and the other cities refused to transfer their gods to Babylon appears dubious as a result. The Persian invasion was imminent, and Sippar wanted to perform its customary cultic ceremonies. As a result, there was not enough time to move the statue to Babylon, or possibly Nabonidus himself had instructed the statue to stay in Sippar, according to Zawadzki. The removal of the monument from Sippar might have been seen as Nabonidus doubting his own success as he planned to stop the Persians a little way north of Sippar.

Cyrus conquered Babylonia soon after the last gods arrived there. Babylonia fell to the Persians rather quickly, despite Nabonidus' preparations, the war lasting less than a month. It is likely that a revolt by a man by the name of Ugbaru—who may have been the designated Babylonian ruler of the province of Gutium— preceded the Persian invasion. Ugbaru overthrew Nabonidus, joined Cyrus, and was appointed commander-in-chief of the Babylonian expedition. Depending on when it occurred, Nabonidus's return from Tayma may have been influenced in part by Ugbaru's uprising.The first thing Cyrus did was launch an assault on Opis. The battle of Opis resulted in a resounding Persian victory, causing significant damage to the Babylonian troops, and forcing them to withdraw past the Median Wall. Shortly after, on October 10, 539 BC, Cyrus captured Sippar without a struggle, and Nabonidus fled to

Babylon. It is unclear why Sippar gave up without a struggle. It's conceivable that the Sippar officials disapproved of Nabonidus' religious beliefs or believed that the Babylonian loss at Opis rendered any further resistance futile. Given that a tablet from Sippar, which was discovered on October 11—the day after the city fell—was still dated to Nabonidus' reign, there may have been some uncertainty at the time.

The Persian army, under the command of the governor Ugbaru, reached Babylon without a struggle on October 12th. The final tablet with a date for Nabonidus's rule is one from Uruk that is dated to October 13—generally regarded as the conclusion of his reign. Shield-wielding Persian soldiers were tasked with guarding Babylonian temples so that priests might conduct their rituals and services in safety. Cyrus himself arrived in Babylon as its new king on October 29 or 30. Although it is unclear whether the people hailed him as a conqueror or as a liberator from oppression, as Cyrus had claimed, he did gain their approval. The fall of Babylon to the Persians on October 12, which was one day before the last tablet attributed to Nabonidus' rule, or Cyrus's arrival into the city, when Cyrus officially assumed the throne, are two alternate dates for the end of Nabonidus' reign.